HORSING AROUND

Trail Riding

Martha Martin

Crabtree Publishing Company
www.crabtreebooks.com

Crabtree Publishing Company

www.crabtreebooks.com

Author: Martha Martin
Editor: Lynn Peppas
Proofreader: Crystal Sikkens
Editorial director: Kathy Middleton
Production coordinator: Katherine Berti
Prepress technician: Katherine Berti
Coordinating editor: Chester Fisher
Series editor: Sue Labella
Project manager: Kumar Kunal (Q2AMEDIA)
Art direction: Dibakar Acharjee (Q2AMEDIA)
Cover design: Shruti Aggarwal (Q2AMEDIA)
Design: Shruti Aggarwal (Q2AMEDIA)
Photo research: Dimple Bhorwal (Q2AMEDIA)
Reading consultant: Cecilia Minden, Ph.D.

Cover: A rider works with her horse
to finish a competitive trail ride.

Title page: A horse and rider take
part in a competitive trail ride.

Illustrations:
Q2AMedia Art Bank : P27

Photographs:
Cover: Cristy Cumberworth, P1: Emily Wright,
P4: Carien Schippers-www.imagequine.com,
P5: Carien Schippers-www.imagequine.com,
P6: Cristy Cumberworth, P7: Larry Prosor/
Photolibrary, P8: Emily Wright, P9: Curtis
Kautzer/Shutterstock, P10: Carien Schippers-
www.imagequine.com, P11: Thinkstock/Getty
Images, P12: Emily Wright, P13: Stockxpert,
P14: Carien Schippers-www.imagequine.com,
P15: Deanna Ramsay, P16: Cristy Cumberworth,
P17: Carien Schippers-www.imagequine.com,
P18: Lynn Smothermon-Smothermon Training
Center-http://stctrailhorses.com, P19: Deanna
Ramsay, P20: Cristy Cumberworth, P21: Richard
Schramm/Fotolia, P22: Juniors Bildarchiv/Alamy,
P23: Michael Klenetsky/Istockphoto, P24:
Kharlamov Igor Viktorovich/Shutterstock,
P25: Al Braunworth/Istockphoto, P26: Robert
Harding/Robert Harding World Imagery/Corbis,
P28: Cathleen Clapper/Shutterstock, P29: Andrea
Betts-www.rideandtie.org, P31: IIC/Axiom/
Getty Images, Folio Image: Wendy Kaveney
Photography/Shutterstock

Library and Archives Canada Cataloguing in Publication

Martin, Martha, 1967-
    Trail riding / Martha Martin.

(Horsing around)
Includes index.
ISBN 978-0-7787-4982-0 (bound).--ISBN 978-0-7787-4998-1 (pbk.)

    1. Trail riding--Juvenile literature. I. Title. II. Series: Horsing around
(St. Catharines, Ont.)

SF309.28.M37 2009   j798.2'3   C2009-903883-8

Library of Congress Cataloging-in-Publication Data

Martin, Martha, 1967-
  Trail riding / Martha Martin.
    p. cm. -- (Horsing around)
  Includes index.
  ISBN 978-0-7787-4998-1 (pbk. : alk. paper) -- ISBN 978-0-7787-4982-0
(reinforced library binding : alk. paper)
  1. Trail riding--Juvenile literature. I. Title. II. Series.

SF309.28.M27 2010
798.2'3--dc22
                                                    2009024757

Crabtree Publishing Company

www.crabtreebooks.com   1-800-387-7650

Published in Canada
Crabtree Publishing
616 Welland Ave.
St. Catharines, ON
L2M 5V6

Published in the United States
Crabtree Publishing
PMB16A
350 Fifth Ave., Suite 3308
New York, NY 10118

Published in the United Kingdom
Crabtree Publishing
Maritime House
Basin Road North, Hove
BN41 1WR

Published in Australia
Crabtree Publishing
386 Mt. Alexander Rd.
Ascot Vale (Melbourne)
VIC 3032

Contents

Trail Riding 101

Competitive trail riding (CTR) combines the thrill of competition with the joy of riding a beautiful animal on the outdoor trail. It's a real team sport. The team is made up of an animal and a rider!

In CTR, the horse and rider team should finish in the best condition within the time allowed. A horse and rider must work well together. They must keep an even pace. They need to handle the challenges of the trail.

Judges include veterinarians and other horse experts. At the start of the ride, each team member begins with 100 points. Points are taken off if the horse or rider breaks a rule.

Creeks and rivers are a challenge for some CTR horses, but they also provide a cool drink and foot soak!

Some trails can be 20 to 90 miles (32 km to 144 km) long. There can also be rides that last from one to three days. In these rides, teams go about 40 miles (64 km) in a day. **Trials** are rides with shorter distances. These allow new riders to practice before trying longer rides.

CTR is a great sport! Riders of all ages and horses of all breeds can compete. It's one of the fastest growing horse sports in the world!

Competitive trail rides can happen anywhere—from a desert to a forest—or even along a country road!

FACT BOX

Riders who are handicapped also succeed in competitive trail riding. Many organizations have special rules. They allow special equipment. This helps riders take part and have fun on the trail.

2 Trail Riding History

Trail riding has been around as long as people have been riding horses. In the Old West, riders often competed to see how far they could go in the fastest time.

At first, riders held casual contests. Speed and endurance were the main goals of those contests. Then things began to change.

CTR riders wanted to have the best long distance riding team. They believed in good conditioning. Communication between horse and rider was important. Riders wanted to find great trail riding **mounts**. Other people would then see what these animals could do.

A group of competitive trail riders created the North American Trail Ride Conference (NATRC). They wanted to promote good **horsemanship** and fair competition.

When a horse and rider work together, they are the ultimate team!

This organization helped make CTR a recognized sport. Soon, other groups began all over the world. Competitive trail rides take place throughout Great Britain, Australia, and Europe. The Canadian Long Distance Riding Association (CaLDRA) encourages long distance riding events.

Some CTR groups focus on a particular breed of horse. For example, the Tennessee Walking Horse Breeders' and Exhibitors' Association (TWHBEA) focuses on the Tennessee Walking Horse.

FACT BOX

Trail riding doesn't have to be a competition. Many people ride trails as a way of seeing the great outdoors. If you want the challenge of a contest, however, competitive trail riding might be for you!

Good guides are really important in recreational trail rides. They help keep the riders safe.

3

Rules of the Ride

Every sport needs to have rules. Competitive trail riding is no different. The rules are made to keep horses and riders safe. Rules are also put in place so that everyone has a great time.

Only healthy and fit mounts may take part in CTR rides. This is a main rule. A nervous or sick horse cannot even try the ride. Riders who mistreat horses are not allowed to ride. A horse can not take drugs to perform better.

Riders and mounts are responsible for following all rules. Competition starts at the **preliminary** check in. Judging begins before the ride even starts. A horse and rider who show bad manners can lose points. Judging continues until the final check-in at the end of the ride.

Give your horse some time to get settled and comfortable before the preliminary check in. It's a good time to catch up with friends, too!

There are different classes of competition. Novice rides are for beginners. Novice riders don't go as far or fast as other classes. The Competitive Pleasure Class is open to riders who are more experienced than novice riders. The Open Class is for serious competitors. It includes longer distances and a faster pace. In the Novice and Open Class, there are different groupings. These include heavyweight, lightweight, and junior riding teams.

FACT BOX

Junior riders in the Open or Novice Classes are riders between the ages of 10 and 17. They have no weight requirements as long as they are in the junior category. They must wear approved safety headgear while mounted. They can not ride **stallions** in competition.

4 Training

All successful athletes need to train. This is true for competitive trail riding teams. A horse and rider must work hard to be ready for a long trail ride.

First, a veterinarian must check each horse completely. Veterinarians can tell if the horse is in good shape and able to handle the physical challenges of CTR. A trainer slowly begins training their horse at least four to six weeks before the ride. A horse that is new to the sport needs to build up endurance. Riders first train horses on a **lunge line**. They begin riding three to five miles (five to eight km) about four times a week.

It's necessary to train in all kinds of weather. Your horse needs to know what to expect!

Riders ride their horses over slopes and different types of ground. They practice going over barriers or things that might scare their mount. A good CTR horse should be able to stop suddenly and back up easily. It must be able to perform a side pass, or a step to the side. Trail horses must learn to eat and drink while on the trail. They can't afford to be fussy! With hard work and practice, riders and their horses will be ready for their first event.

FACT BOX

Riding for hours is hard on a rider as well. A rider needs to exercise regularly too! Yoga and strength-training are great ways to get in shape.

Riding on all kinds of ground is great exercise for your mount's lung power and stamina.

5 Equipment

Winning athletes need the right equipment. In CTR, the condition of your **tack** and equipment can affect your score! What is a well-dressed trail riding team wearing this year?

A good saddle is one of the most important things for the rider. It should fit the horse perfectly. It must be comfortable for the rider. There isn't one suggested brand or type in CTR. It should suit the rider and the horse!

A successful CTR team has the right equipment to make sure both horse and rider are safe and comfortable on the ride.

helmet

layered clothing

water bottle

footgear

The mount will need riding tack. This includes reins, bridle, and stirrups. It is best to choose tack that is comfortable for your horse. There are rules about leg gear. Horses must be bare-legged for CTR. Many riders worry about leg injuries. A rider can choose to use leg bandages or boots on a mount. However, this will cost the rider some points.

The clothing a rider wears on the trail is important. A rider needs to wear layers of clothing. Layers can be taken off or put on in case of changes in temperature. Clothing should be comfortable for the long hours in the saddle. Raingear should be tied to the back of the saddle. Wearing a helmet is suggested for most riders. It is required for junior riders.

Bandanas come in every color! Take your pick!

FACT BOX

A bandana isn't just for the Wild West! A rider can use this triangle of cotton to keep ears warm or wipe down a hot horse. It can also become a rope, a bandage, or a trail marker.

Riders should also carry bug spray and sunscreen. Water or energy drinks are great to have as well.

13

6

Judging the Horse

A horse's fitness is really important in CTR—before, during, and after the ride.

Before a race, each rider presents his or her mount to the veterinary judge. The veterinary judge checks the horse's medical records. A horse without all its shots can't compete. The veterinary judges check the fitness of each horse.

Horses are judged in three areas. These are condition, soundness, and trail abilities and manners. In the NATRC, condition makes up 40% of the horse's score. Things such as pulse, respiration, and gut sounds are carefully checked as part of condition.

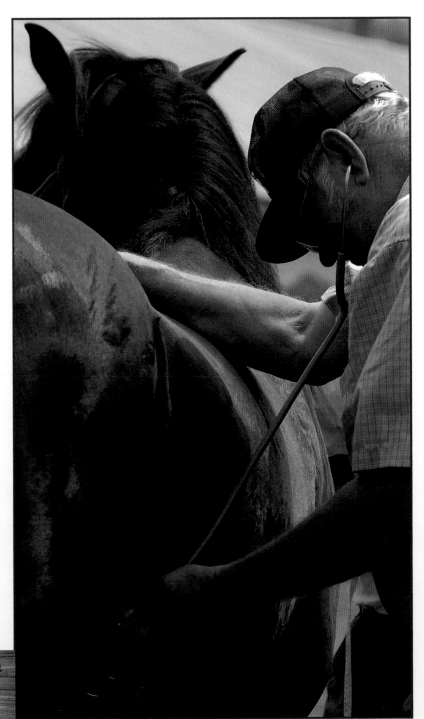

A veterinary judge uses a stethoscope to check the condition of the mount.

Soundness counts for 45% of the score. It shows how the horse is affected by the ride. Judges look for things such as sores on the horse's legs. They check on the horse's "way of going." If it stumbles or trips, its "way of going" is scored low. The last 15% of the score goes to trail abilities and manners. Judges rate how the horse behaves throughout the event. The horse's body language and trail skills are rated here.

A real scorecard from the Seoul's Corners Competitive Trail Ride on June 7, 2009.

Judge RW	OCTRA CTR Scorecard					Weight 220		No. 40	

Ride Seouls Corners	Date June 7/09				Distance 31		Division Open		

Base Pulse Rate is 44 bpm	Pre-Ride	Vet Check #	Vet Check #	Vet Check #	Vet Check #	Vet Check #	Vet Check #	Final Vet Check (4 min / 30 min)	Points
Arrival Time		1158						327 / 357	
Time presented for pulse	62	1204/32						5 / 7	2
Pulse (.25 pts per 2 beats over 44) — 4 min									
Pulse — 10/30 min									
Pulse — Initials									
CRI (beats in 15 seconds) Not Scored		12 / 10							
Trot out – Scored at all vet checks									

Lameness — Grade I pts 3 / Grade II pts 12 / Grade III - Elim.	Not Scored	Scored A	Scored	Scored	Scored	Scored	Scored	A	
Impulsion — A - No Reduction – 0pts / B - Slight Reduction – 1pts / C - Moderate Reduction –5pts / D - Severe Reduction - Elim	Not Scored	A						A	
Presentation — A - Straight, Controlled – 0pts / B - Inconsistent lines – 1-3pts / C - Difficult to evaluate – 4-5pts / D - Unable to evaluate - Elim Comments:	A	A						A	
Mucous membranes — A - Normal, Pink, Moist - 0pts / B - Pale, Tacky – 3 pts / C - Dry, Purple, Brick Red, Toxic line - 10pts or Elim.	Not Scored A	A						A	
Capillary Refill — A - Normal 1-2sec – 0pts / B - Moderate – 3 sec. – 3pts / C - Severe - > 3sec. – 10pts or Elim	Not Scored A	A						A	
Jugular Refill — A - Normal 1-2sec – 0pts / B - Moderate – 3 sec. – 3pts / C - Severe - > 3sec. – 5pts or Elim	Not Scored A	A						A	
Skin Tent (hydration) — A - Normal, Slight – 0 pts / B - Moderate - > 1-2sec. -3pts / C - Severe - >3sec. - 6pts or Elim General Health	Not Scored A	A						A	
Gut Sounds — A - ≤ 2 quadrants minus – 0 pts / B - ≥ 3 quadrants minus/1 null – 3 pts / C - ≥ 2 quadrants null - Elim.	+ + / + +	+ +	+ +					+ + / + +	
Anal Tone — A - Strong reflex - 0 pts / B - Weak reflex - 2 pts / C - Flaccid reflex - 5 pts or Elim.	Not Scored A	A						A	
Total Points per check									

Thumps, Inversion (temperature over 39.5 Degrees Celsius(103 Degrees Fahrenheit)) , Tying up, General Health Conditions: Hydration, Jugular Refill , Anal Tone , Other _____   Eliminate ☐

Final Scoring

Time in	323	Penalty Points – This side	2	Total Points (this side):	
Time out	930	Penalty Points – Opposite Side	—		Total Points (Both Sides)
Elapsed	347	Time Penalty Points	—		
		Total Penalty Points	2		
				Placing	3

7

Judging the Rider

In CTR, a rider's manners really matter. Riders are judged on the way they handle themselves as well as their horses—and respect is key.

The first 20% of the rider's score under the NATRC is based on grooming, equipment, and in-hand presentation. Judges rate these things before the ride begins. In the second area, 50% of the score is given for trail-riding skills such as control and balance. In the last area, 30% of the score deals with a rider's trail manners. Judges also check how well a rider has cared for the horse on the ride.

Some horses really enjoy "showing off" for the judges. Others aren't quite as excited!

The judges try to be everywhere on the trail. They may stop riders to test them on a skill such as dismounting. Sometimes judges hide at places where they expect the horse and rider to face challenges. A stream or ditch could be difficult for some teams. The judges keep their eyes on the horse and rider.

Judges may bring another person with them. The other person writes down information. That person uses special codes or letters to get the information down on the scorecards quickly. All organizations have very strict guidelines that the judges must follow in order to participate.

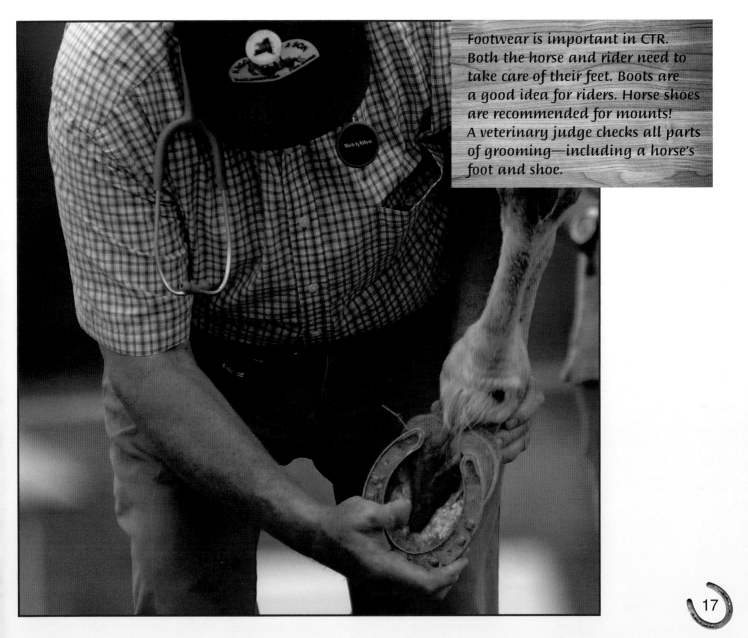

Footwear is important in CTR. Both the horse and rider need to take care of their feet. Boots are a good idea for riders. Horse shoes are recommended for mounts! A veterinary judge checks all parts of grooming—including a horse's foot and shoe.

8

Your First Ride

Riders and their horses have trained and practiced. They feel they are ready for the big event. What can a first-time competitive trail rider expect?

Most competitive trail riding events are held on weekends. People have time for longer rides then. Some people travel miles or kilometers to get to an event. Often pairs ride together. As they ride alongside more experienced riders, new riders learn the ropes of CTR. They ask questions. Trail riders are always a friendly group.

When riders and their mounts arrive at the event, the first thing they do is check in. Here they receive an information package. This includes where to set up the horse and rider's supplies and a copy of the rules.

Competitive trail riding events are like big family reunions— only with horses!

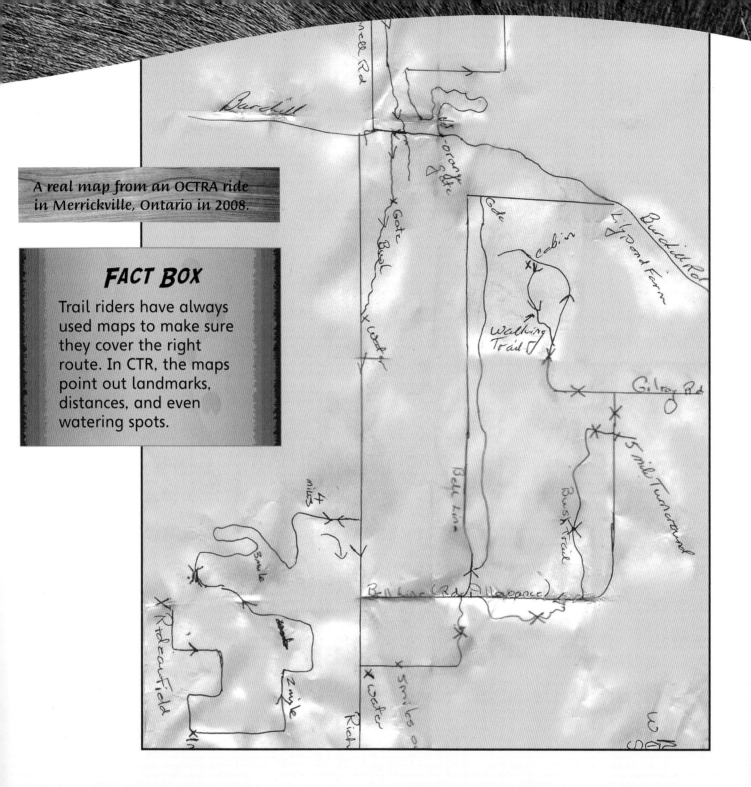

FACT BOX

Trail riders have always used maps to make sure they cover the right route. In CTR, the maps point out landmarks, distances, and even watering spots.

Riders also receive a map of the trail and a schedule. These are both important to have!

The next check will be with the veterinary judge. From this point on, horses and riders are now officially competing. They make sure they look their best. Riders competing in CTR meet new friends and face new challenges. They must check in along the trail and at the end of the ride. Riders make sure to attend the awards ceremony—their team just might be the winners!

9 Problems on the Trail

A lot of things can stop a great team on a competitive trail ride. Unfortunately, even the most prepared teams will sometimes run into situations that can cause problems.

Dehydration is one of the most common problems faced in CTR. Your horse should know to drink whenever water is available. Sometimes that isn't enough. A condition called "thumps" is a problem that can happen when a horse is dehydrated. "Thumps" is caused by an **electrolyte** imbalance. Some trail riders offer electrolytes to their mounts in their water or even better in their feed.

Overheating is another problem. Overheating, or becoming too hot, can cause a horse to become dehydrated and tired.

The best way to stop dehydration is to make sure your horse—and you—take a lot of cooling drinks on the trail.

Even a horse in great condition can be tired after taking part in a CTR competition.

A horse in good condition will handle humidity and heat best. Keep your horse as cool as possible. Give it plenty of water to drink and sponge baths.

"Monday Morning Disease" can also happen on the trail. A horse's muscles begin "tying up." They can get stiff and cramp. The horse may not want to move. This is caused by a combination of things. Overworking an unfit horse is one cause. Giving a horse food with too many carbohydrates is another.

A frightened horse can also be a problem on the trail. It can panic and take off, leaving its rider in the dust.

FACT BOX

A number of plants are actually poisonous to a horse that eats them. It's important to know which ones you might find on your trail ride. Keep your horse safe!

Best Breeds

Competitive trail riding is one of the few horse sports that does not focus on just one breed of horse. In fact, a good trail riding mount doesn't even have to be a horse!

Any breed or mixed breed of horse can participate in CTR. Examples are mules and ponies. Arabians and part-Arabians often rule these events. There are many different breeds of horses on the trails.

Thoroughbreds and Arabians are picked for CTR all over the world. Their **stamina** and athletic ability make them perfect for the trail. The Tennessee Walking Horse has a smooth **gait**. That gives a rider a comfortable trail ride. Morgan horses are also good choices. These animals are hardy and willing to go anywhere.

Ponies make great choices for CTR mounts, especially for young or small riders.

Standardbreds can go all day at a fast trot. They are very calm and steady. Standardbred and Arabian crosses are becoming popular in CTR. In Great Britain, the Welsh Pony is a popular choice. It can handle the trail well and doesn't trip or fall. All ponies make good trail mounts, especially for beginners and lightweight riders.

Mules are a mix of a donkey and a horse. They bring the best of both animals to a trail ride, with great strength and a good nature.

Which breed is best? The one that riders are most confident and comfortable with. Everyone has a favorite. A fit horse that loves the trail is the perfect mount for any rider.

FACT BOX

Mules are born from a female horse and a male donkey. The word "mule" comes from the Latin word, *mulus*, which means the offspring of two different species. Hinnies are just the opposite. Their mothers are female donkeys, and their fathers are stallions.

Mules are known for their ability to handle long distances and heavy loads. This makes them great CTR mounts!

Long Distance Events

Competitive trail riding isn't the only long distance sport to try. There are plenty of other great choices for horse-and-rider fun on the trail!

In many countries, endurance races are held at CTR events. Many people think of them as part of cross-country. The goal of an endurance race is to finish. Your timing is less important. In fact, the motto of endurance racing is "To finish is to win!" The sport of ride & tie is also included at many CTR events. In R & T, a team is made of two riders and one horse. It is a relay event. The riders take turns. One person rides the horse, then stops and ties the horse to a tree. That rider takes off on foot. The horse waits for the other rider of the team to come along.

Competitive Mounted Orienteering takes you to all sorts of interesting places. You never know what you'll find!

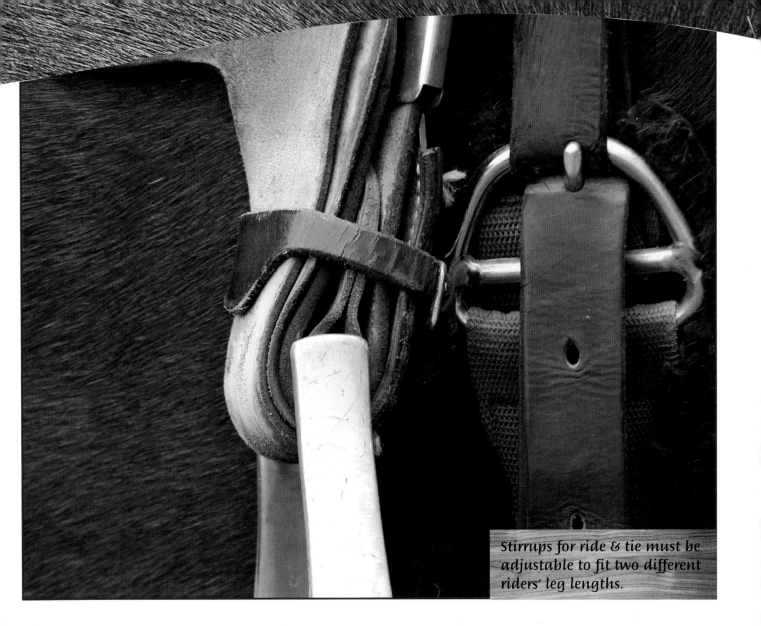

Stirrups for ride & tie must be adjustable to fit two different riders' leg lengths.

That person rides the horse to the next point on the trail. This goes on until the riders and horse reach the end of the trail together. A horse in R & T needs to be well trained! It must be able to stand alone on the trail and wait for its rider to show up.

Another option is called Competitive Mounted Orienteering. Riders use maps to find hidden items in a wilderness area. Clues are given, and individuals can compete alone or in groups. It is like a scavenger hunt on horseback.

FACT BOX

The sport of ride & tie requires special equipment. Stirrups must be adjustable to fit two different riders' leg lengths. Riders also need shoes or boots that work for both running and riding. Companies have invented running shoes with heels for ride & tie!

Famous Trail Horses

Two early trail horse heroes weren't official CTR champs, but they sure did make history. And speaking of history, old Elmer Bandit is still making CTR history at 38 years of age!

In 1925, two horses from Argentina named Gato and Mancha became the first long distance horse heroes. They belonged to A. F. Tschiffely, a teacher who lived in Argentina. Tschiffely wanted to travel on horseback from Buenos Aires, Argentina, to Washington, D.C. The distance was over 10,000 miles (16,000 km). He bought the two horses because he knew the Criollo breed could handle the challenge. Two-and-a-half years later, they finished the trip. They faced every kind of danger. The horses did a great job. Tschiffely decided they deserved their freedom.

Criollo horses come in a number of colors.

This map shows most of the trail Gato and Mancha followed to Washington, D.C.

He took them back to Argentina and set them free.

Elmer Bandit is a modern trail horse hero. He is 38 years old. He's the oldest CTR mount in North America. His owner, Mary Wood, has been competing with Elmer since 1976. In 1986, he was inducted into the NATRC Hall of Fame. In 2008, he broke the record for the most competitive trail miles traveled. He went more than 20,590 miles (33,000 km). Today Elmer has some sight problems and **arthritis**. Even so, Elmer Bandit is going strong!

Trail Riding Champs

Catherine Hogan and Sara Howard are trail riding role models. They have shown the world what hard work and determination can do. In a sport where discipline can mean winning or losing these women are champions.

Catherine Hogan's life changed when she could not walk after a rugby accident. Then a miracle happened. She got back the use of her legs within three months, but her hands and balance were still affected. Catherine needed **physiotherapy** to help her get stronger.

Ribbons and trophies are great, but the best reward is knowing you and your horse succeeded together.

She'd always liked horses so she thought she'd give trail riding a try. Today Catherine and her faithful companion, Dancyn Dream, are trail riding experts! Dancyn has special equipment to make riding easier for Catherine. He is calm and seems to understand her needs.

Sara Howard is also a champion. She is the youngest ride & tie World Championship winner, ever. She's also the fourth woman to win in the history of the sport. In 2008, Sara and her father rode and tied their winning horse, Magic Sirocco, in record-breaking time. They made it into the record books. Since Sara trained Sirocco herself, she was thrilled when he helped make her a champion.

FACT BOX

Sara and her father both love to run long distances. Their running skills helped them win the ride & tie event. If you love running and you also love horses, maybe you should try ride & tie!

Sara and her father are ride & tie champs!

29

Facts and Figures

By now, you know the sport of competitive trail riding is full of record-breakers, history-makers, and risk-takers. Here are some CTR fascinating facts that have helped make the sport terrific!

For many years, a horse named Wing Tempo was the American record holder for competitive distance. He had traveled 20,710 miles (33,329 km). In 2008, Elmer Bandit broke the record and he's still riding today!

CTR is the only sport where you hear phrases such as "Greasy Heel" or "Mud Fever." "Greasy Heel" occurs when a horse has stood in mud for a long time. It is also called "Mud Fever." The horse's heel looks like it has a rash, with sores and raw skin. It sometimes goes up the foot, and is very hard to heal.

The national top point horse in competitive trail riding in 2002 was a Tennessee Walker. Traditionally, the Arabian or half-Arabian breed won that honor. This created a lot of excitement and a little upset too!

The Connemara Trail in Ireland is one of the oldest pleasure trail rides in the world.

One of the oldest known CTR riders is a California man named Bert. Bert turned 99 years old on Feb. 14, 2009. He rides a seven-year-old fox trotter mare. Until 2007, he rode in the Rose Parade each year!

Riders enjoy the beauty of the
Connemara Trail in Ireland.

Glossary

arthritis A chronic illness of swelling and pain in the joints

dehydration Not having enough water in the body, because of exercise or sickness

electrolyte Chemicals needed by the body to control its fluids

gait The way a horse or person moves its legs

horsemanship Act of riding and managing horses

lunge line Ropes with clips on one end, used to lead and train horses

mount A horse in trail riding

physiotherapy Therapy on the body to restore its function

preliminary The first set of a series

stallion An adult male horse that can breed to produce foal

stamina Power to continue despite exhaustion

tack Gear used to equip a horse

trials An activity or event; sometimes used to teach or score participants

Index

Printed in the U.S.A.—CG